Too Many Animals

NATIONAL GEOGRAPHIC

OUR WORLD

NATIONAL GEOGRAPHIC
LEARNING

Based on a folk tale from Ukraine
by Sofia Feldman

It is raining!
There is a nice, dry shed.
A butterfly is flying into the shed.

2

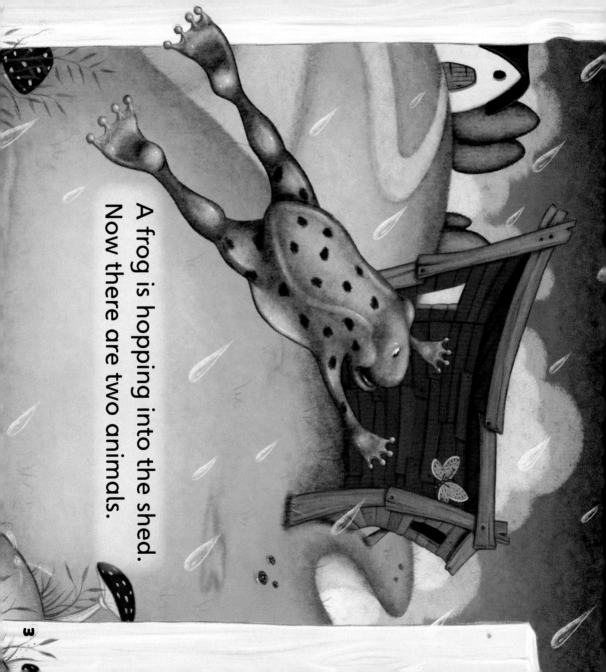

A frog is hopping into the shed.
Now there are two animals.

Two birds are flying in.
Now there are four animals.

4

Two ducks are swimming in.
Now there are six animals.

Two goats are climbing in.
Now there are eight animals.

6

A horse is running in.
Now there are nine animals.

A cow is walking in.

How many animals are there now?

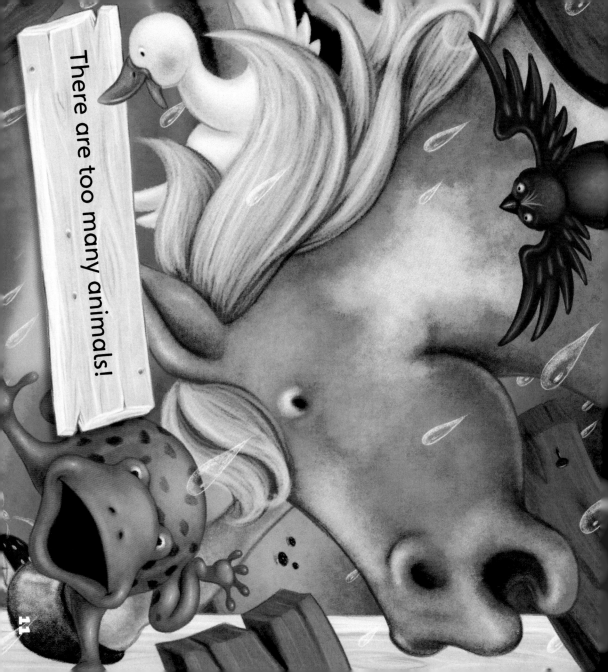

There are too many animals!

11

Facts About Animals

Baby animals usually have special names.

A baby cat is called a kitten.

A baby dog is called a puppy.

A baby duck is called a duckling.

A baby cow is called a calf.

A baby horse is called a foal.

And a baby goat is called ... a kid!

Fun with Animals

Who can do it? Circle the correct animal.

1. A goat / butterfly can fly.

2. A goat / duck can climb.

3. A dog / butterfly can run.

4. A butterfly / duck can swim.

Which animal is it? Write the animal name.

| goat | butterfly | cow | duck | cat | horse |

1. <u>cat</u>

2. _____

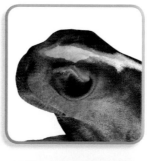

3. _____

4. _____

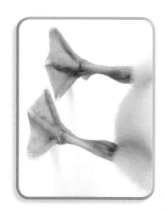

5. _____

6. _____

Glossary

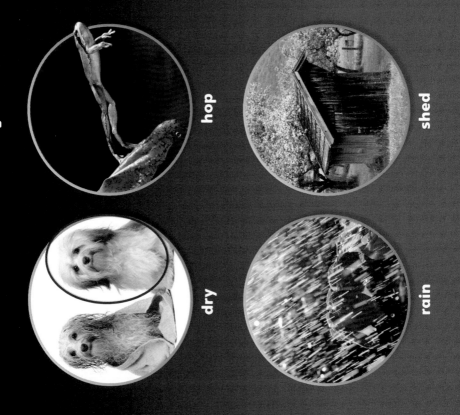

hop

dry

shed

rain